NURTURE

Mentoring is God's invitation to flourish in the love that grows from nurturing and being nurtured. We were made for this!

Polly Balint
PSALM 34:3 NIV

POLLY BALINT

A wholly owned subsidiary of TBN

Nurture

Trilogy Christian Publishers A Wholly Owned Subsidiary of Trinity Broadcasting Network

2442 Michelle Drive Tustin, CA 92780

Cover design by: Trilogy

For information about special discounts for bulk purchases, please contact Trilogy Christian Publishing.

Manufactured in the United States of America

10 9 8 7 6 5 4 3 2 1

Library of Congress Cataloging-in-Publication Data is available.

ISBN: 978-1-68556-847-4

E-ISBN: 978-1-68556-848-1

DEDICATION

For Grace and Mary—
my precious daughters and my mentors.

FOREWORD

For years, every Mother's Day, I would cringe at church if the pastor chose to preach on the Proverbs 31 woman! No one can live up to that amazing, type A, A.D.D., Mary Poppins, for she is more than just practically perfect in every way. She is downright intimidating. And yet, wouldn't we all secretly like to be like that? Or at least have a mentor like that?! I did until I realized that the Lord had supplied loving mentors for me all through my growing years. I just didn't realize it until later, when I could look back and see how many people had a loving, encouraging, guiding, or inspirational impact on me. And then I had a couple of mentors who taught me what not to do—by default! They weren't all the Proverbs 31 woman, or even Mary Poppins, but I learned something different from each one, and I am grateful for all of them. Most of all, my mom!

That's why I love what Polly has done in writing *Nurture*. Her stories remind us of the people God has brought into our lives as mentors, even if we didn't realize it at the time. Looking back over the years and remembering the people, especially the women who have impacted me, makes me realize that mentors come in all shapes and sizes. Some are obvious, some are low-key, some are teachers I had, and some just ooze wisdom upon contact and have a lasting influence. But all of them have helped to shape me into who I am today.

As you read these stories, ask God to reveal to you the people He has put in your life, along the way, to mentor you. Even if you've never had an official mentor, or even a good mother, you will start to see that people have crossed your path who have taught you, inspired you, challenged you, stretched you, or loved you. And you can thank them for being a mentor.

I have been involved in mentorship programs, both professionally and spiritually, and they have all been important. As a member of the Producers Guild of America, I witnessed a professional mentorship program where experienced TV and film producers mentored new producers just coming into the business. Many of the mentees who went on to be quite successful credited their mentors for giving them their break. For a time at the Hollywood Prayer Network, I oversaw a spiritual mentorship program where we matched a mature believer who was an industry professional with a new, young professional who wasn't as strong in their faith. That proved to be a powerful program for everyone involved. The mentors invested in the next generation, and the mentees were inspired to grow in their walk with the Lord as they pursued their careers. It was truly a win/win.

But the woman who was and still is the strongest mentor in my life is my mom. She is now ninety-four years old, and she is the most classy, elegant, loving woman I know. As a teenager, she would bug me about standing up straight and drill me on how to set a proper table. She told me that only truck drivers chewed toothpicks, and shoes must be worn at every meal. She brought me to music and dance concerts, ballets, plays, and movies. We read Shakespeare together, and every time I didn't know the meaning of a word, we would look it up in our family dictionary and then mark the word with a pencil to see if I had to look it up again later. (Some words had four pencil marks by them.) And I would be punished if I ever used the "S" word—"Shut up!" Today, every single morning, she comes to the breakfast table fully dressed, matching perfectly, including jewelry and lipstick. And I can't tell you the number of times through the years she reminded me that my hair would look better with mousse! Sometimes it drove me crazy, but I feel like a lady because of her.

If you have been a mentor or would like to be one, let this book inspire you. If you never had a mentor, why don't you be one when you finish reading this book? We all have something to offer. God created a circle of life, and from birth to death, we all have something to offer others to make the world a better place. Be a mentor to someone else and be sure to thank your mentors, so they know that they made a difference. In fact, I'm going to tell my mom tomorrow that I so appreciate her. Thanks, Polly!

—Karen Covell
Film Director and Founding Director
The Hollywood Prayer Network
Hollywood, CA

REVIEWS

It's hard to describe how much I love these stories! Polly Balint's beautiful tributes to her birth and spiritual mothers make me feel as though I've shared a lemonade, or yummy egg salad sandwich, with them.

I know the source of Polly's joy is the Lord, but now I have a better idea why she is such a beautiful daughter of the King. If ever there was a joy-filled, godly woman, it's Polly! She may not know it, even though we don't spend the time together that most do, but she is a spiritual mentor to me. Her wisdom and joy are invaluable and contagious and are beautifully expressed in these touching tributes.

Polly lives and breathes the qualities she's gained from her spiritual mothers, and I'm quite sure she serves in that capacity for many in her life. This book is such a beautiful reflection of Polly's heart for the Lord and the blessings that can come from a relationship with a spiritual mentor. Her stories will encourage you and inspire you to pray for God to reveal to you such precious relationships that make an eternal difference.

Our Heavenly Father always provides, praying we will be faithful to His calling on our lives and seek His wisdom through a beautiful saint like Polly had.

—Candi Hannigan
Executive Editor
Aroundabout Local Media, Inc.
Woodstock, GA

In a day where encouragement and enlightenment are gravely needed, Polly comes along with her lighthearted but sincere stories and does just that. She opens her world in a raw way and allows you to see how she navigates each moment with godly truth shared by another godly woman, a mentor in her life. In a refreshing way, Polly invites the challenge for you to pour into a younger soul while soaking in the lessons from a richly experienced "mom."

—Susan Reznor Moone CFP®, AIF®
Financial Advisor and Owner
Five Talents Wealth Management, LLC
Canton, GA

The first thing that came to my mind after reading this manuscript was the song 'Precious Memories' and how they mean so much. The words made me feel those precious memories Polly has for her spiritual mothers. I then began to think about my spiritual journey and the spiritual mothers who have mentored me and raised me. How very blessed I am! This manuscript also encouraged me to pray for a spiritual daughter of my own and to seek God and to pray for His guidance as I go about doing the things He wants me to do for Him. I can't wait to read the entire book!

—Michelle Evans-Pirkle
Owner of Ball Ground Beauty Spot
Ball Ground, GA

Reading Polly's true stories of women who have molded her will inspire you. It did me. Polly's gift of developing word pictures allows you to smell her mother's Estée

Lauder and taste her egg salad sandwiches on soft white bread. She allows you into her world to teach you the gentle art of passing on your faith in God's plan for your life through action, kindness, and regular interaction with women who cross your path searching for that light in the darkness. Polly's spiritual mothers and Polly pass along the secret of teaching others how to keep the faith and stay strong, wrapped up in a soft blanket with hot chocolate and a warm hug. I have read all of Polly's books and am proud to call her my friend. You'll become her friend, too, once you start reading her writing. She gives you a glimpse into her soul, and she's beautiful!

—Diane Oberkrom
Owner & Baker
The Soul Food Market
Canton, GA

For all of us who yearn for meaningful connection, this book boldly reminds us that we are called to be spiritual mentors to younger generations. It also reminds us to seek out women of God for direction and encouragement. Life is hard, and God knew we, as women, would need each other. It's great to be reminded of the beautiful plan God had in mind for us as we learn and experience what the Titus woman is all about in this fun-loving book that digs into this ancient concept and how it can enhance our modern lives and fill in the empty gaps we all struggle with.

—Kelley Riddle
Owner & Director
Hickory Flat Dance Academy
Canton, GA

ACKNOWLEDGMENTS

To my beloved husband and best friend, Don, thank you for your unconditional love. You remain a godly, steady example of Christ's tenderhearted, faithful shepherding of those under your care. Thank you for your patience and perseverance in encouraging me with your wise counsel in organizing this manuscript. And thank you, especially, for every time I got frazzled when I couldn't figure out how to correct the bump in the road I created on my laptop. Most of all, you make sure I know I'm loved. I pray I do the same for you! I love you, amazing man of God!

Thank you to my faithful friends and family who love me, encourage me, and have prayed me through to see this dream become a reality in my life. I hope you all know how much I appreciate you and love you!

A very special thanks to the Trilogy Christian Publishing Team, who beautifully led me through this whole process: Acquisitions Executive Shelbi Chandlee, Project Manager Rachel Hiatt, Designer Amanda King, and World Mission Media editing team. Oh, what beautiful things are created when the body of Christ comes together with God-given gifts, skills, talents, and abilities!

Thank You, Lord, for giving me another desire of my heart! I love you, Abba!

CONTENTS

AUTHOR'S INTRODUCTION

A spiritual mother is a mentor. She's the type of gift money cannot buy. She is a love gift from God. The concept comes from Scripture, "Older women are to be reverent in the way they live...to teach what is good. Then they can train the younger women...to be kind, so that no one will malign the word of God" (Titus 2:3–5).

Mentoring is God's invitation to see Him more vividly through a supernatural weaving of hearts. He is inviting generations of women to nurture and to be nurtured. We were made for this!

For some reason, God graciously provided me with *two* spiritual mothers over a span of four decades. He just brought them into my life, and I assumed most Christian women have a spiritual mother. That is until I learned in the Bible studies I was leading that most women have never been blessed with even one, and God sent me two!

All I could think to myself was, "Wow, I must really need a lot of help if God sends me *two* in addition to the gift of having my own mother who loves me unconditionally! Mom was my greatest cheerleader and trusted confidant!"

Spiritual mothers can be any age. What matters is the older woman is to share the wisdom from her own life experiences and teach the younger how to live a joy-filled, godly life. She could, of course, be a mother, sister, aunt, grandmother, or family friend. The relationship could consist of a thirty-five-year-old mentoring a twenty-five-year-old. There are no age rules. It helps if the woman is just a few steps ahead, not only several decades older, like in my experiences. God is creative. He designed this. He will custom fit each one of us with the love and help we need from a mentor.

My experience with my spiritual mothers is that they're women who have been faithful followers of Jesus for decades and have hearts filled with rich, life-giving wisdom and humility. They're fierce prayer warriors because they know God is a mountain-moving God, and it brings Him glory when they pray. They walk closely with Jesus every day because they're fully aware they are sinners who need His help in restoring them from their faults and frailties.

And there's no fanfare with a true spiritual mother. She is trustworthy and not a gossip. She doesn't boast or brag about her wisdom and knowledge. She has a gentle and quiet spirit because the Lord has quieted her soul with His love over the years. She has a beautiful, deep relationship with her Savior. She has the joy of the Lord and a sense of humor because she's learned not to take herself too seriously. She dearly loves her own family and the whole wide world of believers! She is full of life, not pride.

She is usually someone you would not expect to be so filled with a huge dose of Holy Spirit power. But when she walks into a room, she's radiant with God's presence. See, it's not her goal to impress anyone with worldly things like designer clothes, people-pleasing, or her own fame. Her goal is to be spiritually "clothed in strength and dignity" (Proverbs 31:25), and her garments are woven with peace and praise. She is filled with the confidence of Christ's love and light. This describes my spiritual mothers.

The stories I am sharing are about the ongoing, life-giving impact of my birth mom, Mary Elizabeth Gillette Brown, Rosa Evelyn Sorrells Green, and Frances Lucille Park Farley. The purposes of writing this book are to glorify God and to honor the sweet memory of these three very special gifts to my heart. I pray these pages will inspire my sisters in Christ to be praying boldly about seeking out a spiritual mother of their own or become available to mentor a younger woman. It's possible to be a mentor to one or more women and a mentee of another woman more seasoned in the faith! That's been my story!

In the relationship, you both choose what will suit your schedules and how often you will meet. You can decide to work through a Bible study together or simply spend time together by meeting up for a cup of coffee or lunch. Pray and let God lead you both. Let Him blow your mind with His love and magnificent creativity in your new relationship. Maybe you don't live in the same town. There's always social media and cell phones!

Maybe your own mother is a godly woman who loves you unconditionally, prays for and with you, and is your faithful cheerleader! Then praise God for her and thank her! If you don't have a spiritual mother, I urge you to pray for one. Invite one into your life. You won't believe the blessings. And in each of my mother/daughter relationships, God showed me I'm not the only one enriched by the relationship. Over and over, it was obvious to me that each one of my three mentoring mothers *wanted me to come alongside her, too.* I had no idea it could be that wonderful. How glorious is that?

—**Polly Balint**

MOM

My Biggest Cheerleader

When I was playing golf today with three friends, I started thinking about Mom and how she has given me such a wonderful legacy of loving life and even the joys of playing golf. While I was on the course, I started to remember what she was like on my last trip to Coral Gables, Florida, the place where I spent most of my growing years. Mom had to be bathed and dressed. She couldn't walk to the bathroom by herself and couldn't walk anywhere without someone else's arm to lean on. She barely spoke. But she was still so pleasant and cordial and gracious and willing to do whatever was in front of her. She has always been that way, just accepting what she was given with thankfulness and tenacity.

Growing up and even in my adulthood, she always made everything in life an adventure; when we would be eating outdoors and she'd say, "We're having a party!" Whatever it was, she made it special somehow with her words and her attitude. When we were still living on our farm in our hometown of Corry, Pennsylvania, she'd load up a picnic basket, then load us in the station wagon, and we'd drive down a pasture road and then stop by our creek. She'd start a campfire and get out her huge black iron skillet and make us bacon and fried egg sandwiches. We were having another party! Mom saw life as an adventure and always wanted to make the most of every moment with a joyful, thankful attitude.

She even handled the ripple effects of her tragic divorce with so much grace; my dad walked out on her with no warning and left her with their five children. She had the heartbreak of him leaving, and she obviously loved him, and then she faced the relentless struggles of raising five high-energy children. Over the years, I didn't hear her complain about him leaving. I didn't know how deeply she was hurt and how hard it was to care for five rambunctious children as a single mom.

Instead, I saw she was so full of life and love. Every evening she whipped up meals such as huge casseroles, meatloaf, pork chops, baked chicken, spaghetti with homemade tomato sauce cooked with all kinds of spices, including bay leaves. We had huge appetites. When we lived on the farm, Mom often made batches of bread from scratch. Oh, the smells of hot bread! Mom would set one steaming loaf aside from the batch and immediately began slicing and buttering several pieces; the butter was melting on the soft slices, and we were drooling. Together we stood there and relished every hot bite.

She loved us deeply and kept us all together. She made each of our birthdays special with parties with friends and family and giving us our favorite dinner menu requests, presents, cake, candles, and ice cream. She made holidays festive, including Valentine's Day dinners with candy hearts decorating the table.

When we still lived on the farm, we took winter trips to Florida. Years later, when we moved to Florida, she rented large cabins each summer in North Carolina. From my youth and well into my adulthood, we took regular beach trips and countless beachside vacations. We learned to play golf at a young age. We fished. We went boating. We had people over all the time for dinner.

This photo is from a fishing trip weekend in the Everglades. Mom took my family, husband Don, and our daughters Mary (center) and Grace, behind their grandmother.

She didn't expect anything from anyone. She just gave from her generous heart and was loved by the lives she touched. She had a natural gift of hospitality and was always delighted to cook huge meals for our family friends who would just drop in at dinner time. They knew Mom would welcome them. She loved to dance and sing to all kinds of music and enjoyed playing the piano.

She loved to eat and told me, "I'm always hungry!" And I asked her, "Why don't you just eat until you're full? She said, "Because I'd be as big as a house!" And then she'd make a funny face.

She didn't think about herself. She didn't care if she got other people's approval. That didn't matter to her. Instead of being a woman who focused on hiding her age, she was always excited to celebrate another birthday and tell others just how old she was! She wasn't impressed with nice things, even though that was the lifestyle in which she grew up. As a teen, one of her birthday gifts was her first car, a convertible, from her parents. They had her initials monogrammed on her car door. She had a pilot's license, went to a private school, lived the country club lifestyle, and still knew how to run a farm. She wasn't a snob. She just wanted to love people and make them feel good.

She had the kind of faith that believed God was real. She simply believed God could do things that she couldn't. From our earliest years, she made sure we all went to church together, Sunday school and Vacation Bible School, and she always insisted on praying before meals. So, I grew up believing God and Jesus existed, but I didn't have a personal relationship with them. After I became a Christian in my 20s, the power and presence of the Holy Spirit were living inside of me, gently leading me in truth. I had a supernatural relationship with God the Father, God the Son, and God the Holy Spirit. But I'm sure now that God used Mom as my adored role model and His instrument in my life to begin to show Himself to me. He knew I deeply loved her from my earliest years and wanted to be like her. God and Jesus meant something special to her; that's all I knew.

But when I was playing golf today and thinking how calm she was when I last saw her in Florida and she just accepted what was going on: her body failing and not being able to take care of herself. It made me think that is the kind of abandonment God desires for each of His children, to just hand over our lives to Him and trust and believe He will take care of us…and reminded me personally, He will take good care of me. That's the way she lived. She lived an abundant life. God gave that to her. God did it.

A few years ago, she came to visit us at Woodmont Golf & Country Club community and stayed with us a few days. She was being medicated due to her heart weakening and dementia. We were sitting on the sofa in our family room. And yet she said, clearly and succinctly, "This house is you, Polly. This is where you belong. I'm glad you're living here in a golf club community, and your family should be using the tennis courts and the pool and go to the club for dinner! You should be playing more golf; you love to play golf, and you play so well! What do you need? What can I do for you? What can I give you?" I said, "Nothing, Mom. I have everything I need." She just sat beside me and hugged me. She was overjoyed.

While we were sitting there, a major golf tournament was streaming on the flat screen over our fireplace. Then she started talking about golf and being spiritual. It was the most she'd ever shared with me about her faith! She said that she didn't think about golf without thinking about God because He is in everything, and it is very, very important to her. She continued, "Knowing God is everywhere and in everything is of the utmost importance to me. I know I'm a lot older than you, but when God tells me to do something, I say, 'Yes, I'll do it!' And when He tells me not to do something, I will not do it. He speaks to me, and this is very important to me. I think this is right, and it is Him who is talking to me. I want this for all of you—to pray to God and do what He says—and I pray for all of you, too. I know to do that, and then I wait to see what God will do about the matter."

She asked me if I felt that way, too. I wholeheartedly agreed with her. I was in awe and delightful wonder of God's goodness that He would let me hear her say these words! When I showed her the Woodmont Ladies Bible study photo album I created, she got tears in her eyes. She was so happy to know I was leading Bible studies. She kept telling me, "It's you! It's you!"

She loved it. She loved it that I'm a freelance writer, too. She acted so pleased to know what God is doing with my life. It is as if she prayed this all along! Maybe that's what this is all about; maybe God is showing me I'm living the life she prayed for me, and that's why she was so happy about it.

As I look back now, I can see what I couldn't see before I was saved by God's grace. As I began to get into my late teens, I wondered…how in the world could Mom possibly do all she did for us with so much love, joy, and vitality? She had so much pain, heartache, and personal struggles.

There is only one right answer. God was working out His sovereign plan, and He was Mom's strength. God blessed and helped Mom do what she loved doing: loving her family and loving life. And oh yes, loving golf and the beach!

Estée Lauder & Egg Salad

Early one morning, during my daily workout of praying while walking up and down the steep sidewalks that overlooked the neighborhood golf course, I caught a glimpse of the tenth fairway. There was just enough sunlight piercing the grey clouds to make the dew glisten on the manicured grass.

The steep slope of the fairway and the early morning dew still soaking the grass were reminiscent of something I hadn't thought about in a long time. I was taken back to the time when my mom, Mary Elizabeth Gillette Brown, started a junior golf program in our hometown of Corry, Pennsylvania.

Oh, it was a very sweet memory that popped in my head when I looked down the hilly fairway that morning. Memories were growing, and I recalled details. As young children, we'd play very early each Tuesday, and the grass was always as dewy when we started as it was on the tenth fairway this morning! We lived on a farm, and I can still remember Mom getting all five of us sleepy heads and our little sets of golf clubs into the station wagon to head to the club. We had to get there earlier than everyone else because Mom ran the program each week, and she had to set everything up.

But first, Mom had to load the car with clubs and kids and then gather up the materials she needed to run the playful competition. When she had us in the car, she'd dash back into the house for last-minute prep of our lunch.

We were glad to wait because we were half asleep and she was full of energy, doing what she loved to do!

She would take an entire loaf of bread out of its bag, spread the slices with the egg salad she made the night before, and then carefully stack the sandwiches back into the bread bags and seal them with a twist tie. She usually made an additional bag of sandwiches such as tuna fish, baloney, or peanut butter and jelly.

When Mom got in the car with the bags of sandwiches, so did the scent of her favorite perfume, Estée Lauder. And off we went to the club to play some golf!

Mom was a fun-loving, competitive two-handicap player and absolutely loved to play golf. She was passionate all her life about life, loving people, and about helping young people enjoy golf as much as she did. She began hosting her first junior golf program with her own five children: three boys and two girls. She enthusiastically gave of her time, talent, and love to young golfers all over the town of Corry. She was very successful.

Mom was so helpful and encouraging to golfing families over the years that kids and parents wanted to pin a professional golfer title on her by paying her for her countless golf lessons. She told them she wouldn't take money for golf lessons because she wanted to keep her amateur status.

Mom had a huge fan club. The boys and girls in the summer program bought her a bracelet with a charm that was inscribed *Mom* because that's how they saw her. Every week she joyfully set the pairings of players, divided us into age groups, asked the pro shop for gift certificates for winners of each category, and posted the scores. She loved it, and she loved the people she encouraged!

Mom was founder of all kinds of tournaments in Florida when we moved to Coral Gables: for youngsters, juniors, four-ball events for eighteen-to-thirty-year-olds, including the Florida State Junior Golf Tournament in Lehigh Acres. She initiated the participation of the *Girls'* Event of the International Junior Orange Bowl Invitational held at Biltmore Golf Course. She was the first woman to receive the Florida Section of the PGA Amateur of the Year.

She never received any financial rewards for her countless contributions to the world of junior golf. She never asked for any. She did it for the love of it.

When the summers ended in Corry, Mom packed us up, along with our family dog, and we drove three or four days in our station wagon to our winter home in Miami, Florida. Then we'd head back to Corry for the summer and more junior golf at Corry Country Club.

Here is our family: from left, Mom, my brothers Gary and Jeff, me, my sister Julie, and my brother Bill. This photo looks like we were on one of our road trips from

Pennsylvania to Florida, and Mom probably said, "Let's stop for a few minutes and put our feet in the water!" She had such a love for the beach, and we grew up loving it, too, always enjoying many visits to sandy shorelines, from Cape Cod to Key West. Mom strategically planned those annual southbound trips before the brutal blizzards began to cover northwest Pennsylvania, including our farm.

Her parents, who owned a beautiful home and property next to our farm, also owned a winter home with a swimming pool in Miami. It became our winter home for many years until we made it our year-round residence. But our trips back and forth, including our family dog, must have been so exhausting for her. We were young and antsy in the car, of course, and we took turns sitting in the front seat with her.

I was touched that God would bring all of this to my mind in such detail that morning. He knows I miss Mom, and to think again of the yummy egg salad sandwiches in the bread bags, and the scent of Estée Lauder continues to make me smile and thank God.

I sure do serve a tenderhearted Shepherd.

Not the Hokey Pokey

Why do we say we will commit to something while at the same time we are thinking that if it gets too hard, we'll just walk away? We don't like a commitment that includes both of our feet; let's just have one foot in and the other foot out. And if things get testy, then we'll take the other foot out. If the circumstances become calm again, we might put one foot back into the so-called commitment. We don't want to put our whole selves in! No, thank you, because what if I don't like that dance anymore?

Mom's commitment to caring for us showed up in so many ways. She kept pouring out love. She was very close to her loving parents, and it seems it gave her the freedom to generously love others. After we grew up and moved away, she often wrote wonderful, creative letters, sent us cute, funny cards and little notes to us. Often she included her own whimsical poems and drawings. She sent them to her grown children and to her grandchildren.

Mom was totally committed to loving and caring for me and my four siblings after our dad walked out the door. I was young, four or five, when that happened. He never came back home again. But my mother kept us together like a hen gathers her chicks under her wings. We had issues and struggles from the brokenness without a daddy in our home, but Mom insisted on keeping us together. She must have been exhausted every day from taking care of her large, lively household by herself, but since I was so young at the time, I didn't realize it. She didn't complain that her heart was broken or that she was too tired to take care of us. She kept on nurturing us with her unconditional love. And usually, she was either smiling or laughing. She made a commitment, and God was blessing it.

This is an actual press photo of Mom. Yes, that's a golf club she's holding. When she was a young girl, my grandfather put a golf club in her hands, and her instant delight to play the game never waned for more than seven decades. She became a strong competitor and a tournament champion many times and was approached by golf company sponsors who wanted to financially support her to play on the professional golf tour. She turned down tempting offers and planned to stay with her amateur status. She told them that, as a single mother, she didn't want to leave her children. Why would she turn down an opportunity to be paid for doing something she loved to do? There was something she loved more—her five children.

She dated a couple of men over the years. I remember one man who was a highly successful businessman. When we didn't hear about him anymore, I asked her about him, and she said he wanted to marry her, leave us with a hired nanny, and have her travel with him all over the world. She said she wouldn't leave her children behind. Mom's love and commitment to the five of us were more powerful than all her trials and hardships from being deserted by her husband.

Mom loved all kinds of music. She absolutely loved to sing, and she danced with great rhythm! It only took her hearing just a few notes of a song to get her body to respond to the beat. But I guarantee you her favorite dance was not the Hokey Pokey. She was all *in* and stayed *in* until the end. God made it possible.

As I look back, I can clearly see God was being "a father to the fatherless, a defender of widows" (Psalm 68:5).

He was overseeing our household.

But God

I knew Mom was weakening at the time of my most recent visit to see her at my brother Jeff's home in Coral Gables. It was sweet to be with her, and we were still able to communicate. I didn't know it would be the last time I'd see her face to face here on earth.

But God. My brother Jeff hired a wonderful caretaker to come to their house during the day to help Mom. I told her that Mom used to be so full of joy and vitality and that she deeply loved and cared for all of us. I shared that she absolutely loved the ocean, and she often took us to the beach. The woman said, "Let's take her today!"

I said, "Really? It's okay to take her for a ride to the beach? I'd love to take her!"

She said, "Since she loved doing that, it would be good for her!"

So, I drove the three of us to nearby Biscayne Bay and pulled the car over to the shoreline along the causeway. We helped Mom out of the car and let her see the water and smell the salty air. It was something supernatural God was doing, and I didn't even understand the depth of the gift of that moment until years later.

After I returned home from my visit, I wrote down sweet memories of life growing up with Mom in my journal. I was clinging to those memories as the words flowed onto the pages of my spiral notebook.

Weeks later, hospice care was required to come to help Mom. When my siblings told me her body was days away from completely shutting down, I knew I couldn't catch a flight back there to have a few moments with her; my husband was in ICU in a nearby hospital after suffering two strokes in twenty-four hours. I couldn't leave. I wouldn't leave, and I sensed Mom would want me to stay with him. She knew how much I loved her, and I believe she loved me enough to say I should stay with him in his critical condition.

But God. A thought came into my mind. It seemed like a strange request, but I sensed it was God telling me to ask Jeff to put me on the speakerphone when I called and to put it close to her ear. I wanted to read my journal to her so I could let her know my heart was filled with love and gratitude for her.

Jeff understood my heartbreak that I couldn't be there and was glad to help me. Even though Mom was medicated on morphine and her eyes were closed during her final days, I believed God would make it all possible for her to hear my voice. When I called, Jeff put the phone close to her, and I read my journal pages.

Below is the original that I read to Mom. If you recognize the story, it's because it became the first story in this book, updated with more details, and I titled it "My Biggest Cheerleader."

Before I read the following over the phone, I told Mom how much I loved her, was thankful for her, and for her example of living a life filled with love and joy, despite constant struggles and trials.

When I was playing golf today with three friends, I started thinking about Mom and how she has given me such a wonderful legacy of loving life and even playing golf.

While I was on the course, I started to remember what she was like on my last trip to Coral Gables. She had to be bathed and dressed. She couldn't walk to the bathroom by herself, couldn't walk alone, and barely spoke. She would shuffle to walk, but it took two people to help her. But she was still so pleasant and cordial and gracious and willing to do whatever was in front of her. She has always been that way—just accepting what she was given with thankfulness and perseverance.

Growing up and even in my adulthood, she always made everything in life an adventure. When we would be eating outdoors, she'd say, "We're having a party!" Whatever it was, she made it special somehow with her words and her attitude. When we were living in Pennsylvania on the farm, she would load up a picnic basket, then load us in the station wagon. She would drive us down a pasture road and stop at our creek. She would start a fire and get out her huge black iron skillet and make us bacon and fried egg sandwiches. We were having another party! Mom saw life as an adventure and wanted to make the most of every moment with a joyful, thankful attitude.

She even handled the ripple effects of her tragic divorce with so much grace; Dad walked out on her with no warning and left her with their five children. She had the heartbreak of him leaving, and she obviously loved him, and then she faced the relentless struggles of raising the five of us high-energy children. She didn't complain about our dad leaving. She didn't complain when she had to put food on the table, and we had huge appetites. She loved us deeply and kept us all together. She made birthdays special. She made holidays special. We took trips to Florida. We rented large cabins in North Carolina for the summer. We took regular beach trips and beachside vacations. We learned to play golf at young ages. We fished. We went boating. We had people over all the time for dinner.

One of her secrets is that she didn't expect anything from anyone. She just gave from her generous heart. She was well-loved in the community. She loved to entertain in our home and loved to dance and sing, and loved to eat, especially ice cream! She had quite the gift of hospitality.

Another one of her secrets is that she did not care what people thought of her. She didn't think about herself. She didn't care if she got other people's approval. That didn't really matter to her. She wasn't impressed with nice, expensive things, even though that was the lifestyle in which she grew up. She wasn't a snob. She just wanted to love people and make them feel good.

She had faith in God. But she was very quiet about it. It was like she simply believed. She made sure we all went to church, Sunday School, and Vacation Bible School. A few years ago, she told me she prayed for things and prayed for us, her children, and she would then leave the matter with God and not worry about it after she prayed.

But when I was playing golf today and thinking how calm she was when I last saw her and she just accepted what was going on: her body failing and not being able to take care of herself. It made me think that is the kind of abandonment God desires of me—of all His children—to just hand over my life to Him and trust and believe He will take care of me, He will take good care of me. That's the way she lived. She lived an abundant life. God gave that to her. God did it.

And now He is showing me that I am living the exact life she wanted for me. I didn't realize it until she said, "You should be living in a country club, and you, Don, and the girls should be having their friends come to the club and play tennis, too, and you should use the golf course. You and Don should be going to the club for dinner. You should be playing golf!"

A few years ago, she came to visit us and stayed with us a few days. It was obvious she was beginning to get very sick, and yet she said, "This house is you, Polly. This is where you belong. What do you need? What do you want? What can I give you?"

I said, "Nothing, Mom. I have everything I need." She just sat beside me and hugged me. When I showed her the Woodmont Bible Study photo album I made, she got tears in her eyes. She was so happy to know I was leading Bible studies. She loved it.

She was thrilled I'm a writer, too. She acted so pleased

to know what God is doing in my life. It is as if she prayed this all along! Maybe that's what this is all about; maybe God is showing me I'm living the life she prayed for me, and that's why she's so happy about it!

After I finished reading it, there were a few seconds of silence from the other end. I didn't know what had happened. I kept saying, "Jeff, Jeff, I'm finished reading; that's all of it. Are you there?" I didn't know he had been quietly sobbing while I was reading.

Then I heard, "Polly! Polly! Mother heard you! Mother heard every word! You have captured Mother perfectly! That's Mother!" He was sobbing.

I was sobbing, too, and could hardly read through my own tears. I believed it was God who put it on my heart to call and speak to her during her last days on earth. Somehow, I knew God would help me connect with her for the last time on earth. God gave me that tenderhearted gift because I couldn't be there in person.

But God had prepared more comforting gifts for my breaking heart. Jeff asked me to send him a copy of the journal pages so he could make copies to share with friends who came by to see Mom during her final days. I was glad to do it! And then I found out he shared the pages with the minister who would be leading Mom's memorial service. He asked Jeff if he could read it during the service. I was amazed with that news and deeply moved to more tears. God gave me a sort of presence there to honor Mom!

This photo was taken during my last time being face to face with Mom. But God waited years before He revealed to me the depth of His love in giving such a personal, healing gift. Yes, I was grateful to have this photo of us together, but until just recently, I realized that for our last time together, I was given the overwhelming joy *that, this time, I would take Mom to the beach*!

We should never underestimate the love and power God has for His children. "How great is the love the Father has lavished on us, that we should be called children of God! And that is what we are!" (1 John 3:1)

MRS. GREEN

A Gentle Spirit with Holy Spirit Fire

Mentoring is one of God's gentle, transforming ways to pass the gospel onto the next generation. The key is, we must be willing to participate! Do we care about those who are coming behind us? All of us have someone who is younger than we are—yes, we do! Women in their twenties can encourage teens in the ways of the Lord; eighty-year-olds can share life experiences with middle-aged women as well as with twenty-year-olds. Pre-teens girls can be effective in the lives of girls who are younger.

Our lifestyle is our testimony, and that's what will draw a younger woman to a mentor.

Many years ago, when I became a Christian, I read that a young woman should seek out an older woman who is a godly example and then get to know her and learn God's ways from her. Mrs. Green has been that mentor to me. When I moved from south Florida to Atlanta, I joined a church where my brother, Bill, and his family were members. I soon realized Mrs. Green and her husband, Lowell, were known as a loving couple—toward each other and toward everyone around them. The Greens were respected as fiercely faithful prayer warriors. They fervently prayed for missionaries and regularly traveled to participate in retreats and conferences.

Mrs. Green was seen and known as humble-spirited, faithful in her walk and ways, and everyone knew her and Mr. Green to be pillars in the faith. I sought her out. An incredibly special bond quickly developed between us. God knit our hearts together.

In the early years of our friendship, we began to meet regularly at her home in metro Atlanta. She was widowed by then, and she'd make us lunch, and then afterward, we would pray together. She'd share her heart with me, and I'd share mine with her because of the deep trust that quickly developed between us. We interceded for our families, friends, church, missionaries, the world, our country's leaders, you name it; she wanted to cover it in prayer.

She'd often say, "The hardest thing for a Christian to do is pray!" She showed me a faithful prayer life requires work and time. It is a labor of love—love for God and for those for whom we pray. And yes, it takes time to pray. She was totally convinced from countless experiences in her own prayer life that God can move mountains through the prayers of His saints. She would say, "My dear, if you are going to pray for rain, you need to carry an umbrella!"

But faithful praying takes a commitment of love for

God and love for people. She had such a deep love for God and believed a spiritual revival could come if more of God's people would repent and pray.

Her favorite verse was Philippians 4:6–7. "Do not be anxious about anything, but in everything, by prayer and petition, with thanksgiving, present your requests to God. And the peace of God, which transcends all understanding, will guard your heart and your mind in Christ Jesus." And she often would emphasize "with thanksgiving" when she would recite it. She loved God's Word.

Mrs. Green cared about everybody she encountered. Whether we had phone conversations or meeting in person, she was always interested to stay up to date with the activities and well-being of my husband, our two daughters, and even my extended family. When there was any kind of concern, she always asked me for a prayer update.

In this photo, Mrs. Green is holding our newborn daughter, Mary. Anyone who was close to me knew it was a deep longing of my heart to have children. When I thought I couldn't conceive a child after a few years of trying, Mrs. Green was one of my strong encouragers to keep praying and trust God. She was overjoyed with us when I learned I was pregnant with our firstborn daughter, Grace, and we all celebrated again when I gave birth to Mary!

Mrs. Green used to send me sweet, thoughtful cards to encourage me during special seasons of my life. When each daughter was born, her note included, "I prayed for this child," a verse from 1 Samuel 1:27. She was thrilled God answered her prayers for us, and as she often did, she pointed me to Scripture, this time to the powerful story of Hannah who longed for a child, and God granted her the birth of Samuel!

She prayed for countless others, too, as they asked for prayer and had prayer lists. We would pray together about their calamities and celebrate their praises.

At church, it wasn't unusual for people to approach her in person and by phone to ask her to pray for them. Over decades she has shared herself with countless other *mentees* who desired to be close to her, and they, too, cherished time spent with her.

She made meals for friends in need. She often baked a delicious pound cake for people. She visited her sick friends, and when she couldn't drive herself any longer, she would ask someone to drive her. I was honored to be her personal driver several times and enjoyed it because it meant I spent more time with her.

Every once in a while, after we finished lunch and our prayer time, she'd ask me to drive her to visit one of her dear friends who was paralyzed with multiple sclerosis. Gwen quickly became my friend, too.

Along with having a heart for God, Mrs. Green had a dry sense of humor and a quick wit. I loved to make her laugh. When she'd get her feelings hurt by some situation, she prayed and asked God to help her push any negative thoughts out of her head. She was always quick to ask God for forgiveness in case it was "her fault," she'd tell me.

I attended a small celebration of Mrs. Green's hundredth birthday. Her son, David, and daughter, Anna, hosted a delightful party on Peachtree Rd. in Atlanta, where Mrs. Green lived in an attractive, high-rise retirement home.

At 100, Mrs. Green had some dementia and did not recognize faces easily anymore. She still looked so beautiful and radiant. She often said she is longing to see her Lord and Savior Jesus Christ face-to-face and is very enthusiastic at the thought of seeing "her Lowell" again!

Once an avid reader, she had to give it up. But at her birthday party, she was enjoying her cake. She was on her second piece and enjoying a cup of punch. There was another cut piece of cake on the table, untouched, and she was staring at it. I said, "Do you want another piece of cake?" I was laughing because I knew of her dry wit, and

I said, "You've had two; do you want another?" Someone at the party said, "Hey, she's 100 years old today, and she's Mrs. Green, so she can have anything she wants today!" We all were laughing in agreement, and I pushed the plate in front of her.

Mrs. Green always loved her sweets. Before she weakened to the condition she was in that day, I used to take her to one of her favorite places to eat, Chick-fil-A®, to order chicken noodle soup, crackers, and the famous lemonade. Then just before leaving, I'd refill the lemonade and take it with us so she could sip on it all afternoon. During those lunches, she kept thanking me for taking her there and said it was, "So great to get outdoors again and do this with you."

I can't list all the ways Mrs. Green has blessed my life and the rich teachings that came from watching her persevere and live her life. She loved God with all her heart, and she couldn't keep His love to herself. She was committed to loving and serving Jesus. I believe anyone who really knew her will tell you the same thing. I thank the Lord that He brought her into my life in such a special way! She has left such a glorious legacy for me.

Is God calling you to become a mentor, no matter what your age? Or are you hungry for a mentor and afraid to invite someone into your life? I invited Mrs. Green into mine! Pray and ask God if He's speaking to you to take the first step. Put your foot in the water and see if God will part the sea. If you're willing, then the Spirit of God will take over and eventually knit your heart with your mentor or mentee. That's what happened to me! A supernatural relationship grew from all the love. Since it's Christ-centered, it's healing and empowering! Remember, God designed the Titus 2 principle! It's His plan for us to live it out, for His glory and our good! We really were born for this!

The Witness of a Worthy Woman

Mrs. Green was called *Evelyn* by very few in our congregation. She was a very loving woman with a gentle spirit and yet radiant with the presence of the Lord. Everyone who knew her knew it to be true. She was highly honored and yet remained humble because she was too busy keeping her eyes on her Savior.

Just like the woman described in Proverbs 31:25, Mrs. Green was "clothed in strength and dignity." That's what I observed as one of her three young traveling companions as we were on our way to a four-day Christian retreat. I was just getting to know her after recently seeking her out as a friend and mentor.

This gathering, one of several organized by the Sovereign Grace Fellowship of Clemson University, was to be a time of their graduation celebration in the sun on South Carolina's coastline. Mrs. Green was invited to be their iron-sharpening chaperone.

As we packed the car in her front yard, I thought about how she must miss Mr. Green. He was her beloved husband for forty-two years, who died only weeks prior to this particularly clear spring day. They were popular chaperones at retreats, and this is one that they were invited to every year as dearly loved, spiritual grandparents. The

Greens' personal life mission was that they "sought to love the Lord's people wherever they found them," as Mrs. Green would tell me later during our five-hour drive.

As our car moved down the broad highway and into our adventure, the early Sunday afternoon warmed the windows and sprayed the west side of the gold Chevrolet. The sunshine covered Mrs. Green's tightly curled silver hair and must have soothed her shoulders beneath her well-pressed brown and white checked dress.

As the two of us in the back seat began to unwrap our picnic of ham sandwiches, pineapple and cream cheese sandwiches, soft drinks, and potato chips, I thought of this woman who surprised us with such a bountiful lunch. We didn't expect it, but that's what she told me she used to do when she and Mr. Green would travel to retreats.

Tossed between my hunger for lunch and pangs for the secret of her wisdom and way of life, I quizzed her as I ate. Her voice cracked as she began to speak, but then she boldly described the schedule she shared with Mr. Green and now follows without him. She gets up at 4:30 a.m. to read and meditate on Scripture. "A cup of hot tea will temporarily break the fast until breakfast," she told me.

Overwhelmed by getting insight into her deep walk with Christ, I wondered aloud how she came to know Jesus as her Lord and Savior. She was fourteen when *a high school teacher peppered his lessons with Christianity*. That was the summer she was baptized and made her commitment, according to the Georgia-born grandmother.

She told me that for many years she and "her Lowell" believed the history of the reformed doctrine. "We heard there was a reformed man in Atlanta who had a church. We sought him out. Through daily prayer with Lowell and praying separately, we waited upon the Lord and eventually joined," Mrs. Green carefully recalled this between bites of her last potato chip.

We were finishing lunch and moving on through tiny towns with two-lane roads and stopped once for ice cream. We worked our way through the city of Charleston and pulled up in front of a massive, two-story barracks-like beach house, which is what would be our shelter for our stay.

Clad in bathing suits and Clemson jerseys, early bird arrivals scattered from the beach and house to meet our car. These college graduates were full of anticipation of her arrival. Mrs. Green was greeted with hugs and kisses, as well as condolences for the passing of Mr. Green. They deeply loved him, too.

Well into the evening, new faces and old friends to Mrs. Green filtered in, and by 10:30 p.m., the number of the college-age clan grew to thirty. By then, the singing of psalms and hymns was accompanied by piano and guitar, and desserts were passed around. Mrs. Green smiled, sang, and rocked in a chair brought especially for her by a young friend.

Individually, travel-weary singers sleepily found their triple-decker bunks in the separated men's and women's areas. Mrs. Green and her driving companions were to sleep in the quarters on the first level. The second level housed the two massive bunk rooms, the commercial-sized kitchen, the dining/meeting room, and the long, screened porch which faced the ocean.

Bathing suits and Bibles were the order of the new day as the college graduates, who studied to be nurses, architects, engineers, veterinarians, and business executives, greeted the beach and dunes. As God's children, they rested, knowing they would soon set out in the world as a new crop, a new harvest.

And there was Mrs. Green, watching this through her sunglasses and wearing a plaid dress, sneakers, and neatly combed hair. She was quiet as a prayer and as observant and available as an open Bible. She'd sit in her rocker on the porch for a while. I watched as a tall, brown-haired young man named Mike approached Mrs. Green and sat beside her. He was planning to become a sportswriter. She knew everyone's name and personal and spiritual background by the end of the retreat because they would pull up a chair beside her and talk for almost an hour. A red-haired co-ed, who studied to become a nurse, would join them. They sat on the wooden floor that was sparsely covered in peeling grey paint.

Later, Mrs. Green sat on the long, wooden stairway that leads from the porch to the sand. Several youths surrounded her for advice, for attention, and to honor her because they knew *wisdom has built her house* (Proverbs 9:1).

She strolled to the beach to closely watch six young believers build a sandcastle. And with sand in her shoes, she smiled. Then she sat on a beach towel and visited with a newcomer.

Mrs. Green is *like merchant ships; she brings her food from afar* (Proverbs 31:15). This spiritual feast of the gathering of God's people was sweetly soul-satisfying and spirit-filled.

On the journey homeward, a feeling of renewal came over the car like a wave. Freshness, vitality, and humility on a grand scale is the description of this worthy woman. *"But a woman who fears the Lord, she shall be praised. Give her the product of her hands and let her works praise her in the gates"* (Proverbs 31:30–31).

As we pulled away from the waving crowd, Mrs. Green was putting away some notes she had been journaling throughout the weekend. They were to remind her to keep in touch with and to pray specifically for each one whom she touched.

Beautiful seeds were planted in my heart as I watched the witness of this worthy woman called Mrs. Green. She didn't think about herself or her impact on the adoring students. Her eyes were on Christ and His love.

God blessed our friendship for more than thirty years and nurtured us both with His love and grace. Our all-knowing God knew we were like-minded and hungry for more of Him, so He nourished our souls over and over!

The Titus 2 principle of mentoring is not a one-way street. Mrs. Green said to me, "It is surely of the Lord, Polly, our attraction to each other. Thank you for being so sweet and considerate of me."

I am continuing to enjoy the fruit of this love of God... and of Mrs. Green.

FRANCES

Tiny Frame, Giant Faith

Frances Farley came into my life when she was in her 90s. The spunk and joy of the Lord radiating from the diminutive Frances Farley could not be ignored, not even in the megachurch where both of our families were attending.

Inside the main building on the sprawling church campus, there was a very wide hallway, sort of like a runway, surrounding the massive sanctuary. The first time I saw Frances, she was quickly making her way around the curve toward the women's ministry booth where I was standing with my friend. Frances couldn't weigh hundred pounds, but she stood out from the crowd because she was a fast-moving bundle of energy and joy. We watched her as she passed people who were walking in the opposite direction. She said to each person, "Hello!" "Good morning!" "God bless you!" Her personal greeting always included a smile so big her eyes would squint as if she was sending a personal hug with her eyes.

When she was about to approach and pass by our booth, we laughed and smiled at her in amazement. She noticed we were watching her. She giggled, raised her shoulders to her ears as if to hug us, and said, "God bless you!" She didn't stop to talk, but she giggled again and kept on her way.

She was so tiny and so full of life and love. She made us giggle every Sunday we were there manning the women's ministry booth. She was consistently jetting past us, sending greetings of love with giggles.

During worship in the sanctuary, my husband sang with the 250-member choir, which remained seated on the stage until the service was over. As a member of the congregation, I chose to sit down in front, in the second-row aisle seat, so I could be close to the lively music of the full orchestra. Sometimes I walked in when the wonderful music was cranking up, and people were already standing to their feet to sing. I would already be worshiping and singing as I kept my stride to the beat of the music, making my way to my seat.

While this was going on, I didn't know Frances and her family sat across the aisle and only a few rows back. Then one Sunday, she caught my attention after a service to let me know we sat in the same area, and we began to greet each other every week. There was a definite connection. She would tell me later that she watched for me to come bouncing down the aisle to my seat and that she loved to watch me worship. She would shake her head to emphasize her emotions, and her eyes would get teary. I had no idea that was happening. I just love to worship. God has a beautiful way of drawing people together for His purposes. Frances was a true worshiper, and she saw that in me. I was in awe of God's sending me such a sweet blessing.

Then one Sunday before the service began, she called me over to her and gave me a small piece of paper where she had written her full name, her address, and her phone number. She also drew a little map of her street and the main intersection into her neighborhood. She had invited me into a friendship!

God knew exactly what we both needed in that season of our lives. He provides when we don't even know what we truly need at the time. I had been feeling the deep loss of my own mother and then of the passing of Mrs. Green. They were now in their heavenly home. Then along came Frances!

"Whatcha Know to Tell Me?"

*Delight yourself in the LORD and He will give you
the desires of your heart.*
Psalm 37:4

Frances was my trusted friend, laughing partner, mentor, prayer partner, confidant, and inspiration. Early in our friendship, I often visited her in the home she shared with her husband. She gave me a map, remember? Frances and her husband Don were parents of three grown children, grandparents to four grandchildren, and blessed with five great-grandchildren. They had a lovely home in a nice neighborhood. She and I would meet in the front room of her house, a cozy place off the foyer. There was a long, comfortable couch and soft chairs. Our meeting room wasn't shut off from the rest of the house with a door, but it was like a private place tucked away from the family room and kitchen. I ended up calling it her war room since that was the place she'd go each morning for prayer and Bible reading. And when we talked for long lengths of time on the phone, she sat on the couch with her pillows supporting her back, and a blanket covered her legs and feet. She had a glass of water on the table next to her. Every time I called, she told me she was all situated to talk, and she always said, "Whatcha know to tell me?" She was ready for sharing hearts and a time of prayer. She selflessly asked for specific updates on my family because we prayed for each other. And whenever we ended our conversation, she'd encourage me that she was knocking on the doors of heaven on my behalf by saying, "I'm on my knees! You know I'm on my knees!" And I said it back to her. When we are interceding for others, the Spirit of God is mightily at work, moving mountains that only He can move. We should never underestimate the power of prayer with a trusted, faithful friend. There's a supernatural sweetness when like-minded friends pray together.

So, she knew about my family. Whenever I brought our two-year-old grandson, our daughter Mary's son, by Frances' house so she could see him, tears of joy would leak from her eyes as she talked to him. When our daughter Grace, who lives in Los Angeles, came to town, Frances invited the two of us to have tea. Frances was ninety-four years old at that time. When we walked in her home, she had a table already set with flowers, fine china, and cookies. Then Grace sang for her, and Frances clasped her hands and held them on her chest, and I could see her worshiping as her tears flowed. She often couldn't hide the radiance of her grateful heart.

When Frances and I would connect by phone or in person, we talked about Scripture often and about the love and power of God. We encouraged each other with it. We discovered that we each, personally, liked to start our day reading and praying through Psalm 51 to confess sins and Psalm 139 to draw near to the love God has for us.

I often tried to get her to go out to eat with me, but she turned me down. It was as if she didn't want to ask anything of me. She used to call me her angel. But I told her that's what she is to me.

Then during one of our countless phone conversations, Frances told me she had a coupon for a local barbeque restaurant. She asked me if I wanted to pick her up and we could use the coupon to get a barbecue sandwich, so we made plans to go. After we ordered, she asked them to cut the barbeque sandwich in half and put it on two plates. We sat down across from each other, prayed, and then ate.

She said, "Is this okay? Do you like doing this? This is what my husband and I do. We get a coupon and split the sandwich. Are you alright with this?"

I was loving it. I kept seeing more into her that she truly had a thankful heart and her life in Christ was her joy. What most people saw as an ordinary occurrence— such as eating at a restaurant with a good friend—she saw as a special treat from God. I felt the same way.

She had health issues that kept me from visiting her in the last couple of years of her life. Then global pandemic hit and kept us physically separated from each other. But we didn't let that stop us from spending time together. We would continue to have our hour-long phone conversations, sharing our hearts, laughing, praying, and especially interceding on behalf of our troubled world. Our friendship deepened during the ongoing pandemic— there was so much to pray about.

And as the pandemic continued, I saw her less and less because her health issues were taking over. She couldn't talk on the phone anymore, and Frances was eventually hospitalized. At the age of ninety-seven, sweet Frances was on her way heavenward to the God she loved and delighted in so powerfully.

Frances is deeply missed here on earth, but her legacy of loving Jesus and loving people has touched countless lives. Our relationship has left me with a heart of gratitude to God for such love.

Mentoring is God's idea of inviting women of all ages to be willing to co-labor with Him to spread His love. It's an open invitation to flourish in the love that grows through nurturing and being nurtured. I'll say it again—we were made for this.

NURTURE NOTES

We would be astonished at the supernatural power that would come to us if we began passionately *pressing in* and *pressing on* with Jesus. That's what the woman with the issue of blood experienced in Mark 5:25–34, and that's what I witnessed in my mentors.

You can read more about this passage of Scripture in the first story of Nurture Notes.

God used my mentors to inspire me to draw close to God. They sowed motherly seeds of unconditional love, wisdom, uncanny insight, and they unknowingly discipled me. For each relationship, there was a powerful bond of trust, which created a safe place to flourish as God knit our hearts together. Christ was their confidence; they delighted in Him, which gave them freedom to live and love for God's glory.

When I was young in the faith, I was hungry to know God intimately and started my own personal journey of studying the Scriptures, which begat a passion for truth. I was worn out from believing lies. I devoured God's Word and eventually began writing to share treasures of truth with other women. I thought if I was stuck in a cycle of unbelief (Mark 9:23), abandonment issues (Psalm 68:5), and fear of man (Proverbs 29:25), other women must be struggling, too.

I began leading Bible studies for women to encourage them in the Lord and found myself making the same comment to them during the studies: "I know why you ladies keep coming back each week to the study. I know it's not because of me. It's because women are tired of being lied to about their appearance, their lives, their choices, their families, their lifestyles. You know I bring you the truth because the Scripture is what we are studying, and it is the only truth." And in every study where I shared that thought, it was within seconds the women unanimously were nodding their heads in agreement.

That is what you'll be reading in the following pages, Nurture Notes. The truth of God's Word that sets women free.

When She Heard About Jesus

"...she came up behind him in the crowd and touched his cloak..."

Mark 5:27

Have you heard about Jesus? The woman with the debilitating issue of blood (Mark 5:25–34) surely did.

This woman suffered with massive "bleeding for 12 years...suffered a great deal under the care of many doctors...spending all she had, yet...grew worse" (vv. 26–27). Her condition made her an outcast and was considered unclean, according to Levitical law (Leviticus 15:25–33).

When she heard about Jesus, she was given a gift, a gift of faith. In her frail, sickly condition, she chose to push through the crowds and not let anything or anyone get between her and Jesus (v. 27).

She knew she would have to go into a crowd where people could judge her, or she could fall into destructive gossip from her neighbors. Maybe she would be held back by the lies of the enemy telling her not to go to Jesus for help. She might be intimidated by the fear of opinions of others or by any of the other worldly influences of the noisy crowd.

She made a compelling decision of faith by humbling

herself and wanting to be healed by Jesus. What people thought of her no longer mattered. She had her eyes fixed on Jesus and wanted to get close enough to Him to touch His garment. She would push through crowds to get close enough to Jesus to touch Him so she could be healed. She believed He was telling the truth to the multitudes during His three-year ministry on earth!

"When she heard about Jesus, she came up behind Him in the crowd and touched His cloak because she thought, 'If I just touch His clothes, I will be healed.' Immediately her bleeding stopped and she felt in her body she was freed from her suffering. At once Jesus realized the power had gone out from Him. He turned around in the crowd and asked, 'Who touched My clothes?' Then the woman, knowing what happened to her, came and fell at His feet and, trembling with fear, told the whole truth. He said, 'Daughter, your faith has healed you. Go in peace and be freed from your suffering'" (vv. 27–30, 31–34).

Yes! Instantly, a supernatural transformation took place. It begins with a growing relationship with Jesus. Oh, the life-giving, restoring, healing, saving power of the blood of Jesus is infinite. When He calls us, He transforms us from spiritual death to spiritual life; our old self dies, and we're a new creation! "Therefore, if anyone is in Christ, the new creation has come; the old has gone, the new is here!" (2 Corinthians 5:17)

You know, just like that woman, we have personal issues, too, and we have a choice when we hear about Jesus. But what do we do? Turn our backs on Him because we don't see our need of a Savior? We don't want to change. We're too busy.

Or do we want our lives transformed and revived? Do we want to overcome our personal issues or live with lies? Do we want to believe He is who He says He is? My beloved mentors were not crowd followers. Not one of them was driven by the approval of others. Each of their abundant lives was on paths paved with prayers of faith. In their unconditional love and humility, they stood out from the crowd, made the world a better place for me and countless others. "They lived believing that all things are possible with God" (Mark 10:27).

You know, we, too, can push through the crowd made up of the devil's lies, the comparison trap and addiction of social media, seeking celebrity status, idolatry, gossip, envy, jealousy, selfishness, worldliness, fear of man, pride, unforgiveness, and unbelief! Maybe our priorities will change, and our lives will wholeheartedly glorify God. Maybe just like that healed woman experienced, a Holy Spirit-driven passion will rise in us, and we'll refuse to let anything or anyone keep us from drawing close to Jesus. That's when we discover a supernatural relationship with Jesus is what we've longed for all along!

His blood was her cure. She was "lavished with God's grace" (Ephesians 1:7) because she pushed through the crowds of people-pleasing distractions to get close to Him.

His blood was her cure.

"He said to her, 'Daughter, your faith
has healed you. Go in peace and be freed
of your suffering.'"

Mark 5:34

God Wants Us to Know

"...how wide and long and deep is
the love of Christ..."
Ephesians 3:18

God wants His children to know how much He loves us. He sees us struggle. He wants us to know His love so we can be free to live and love abundantly for His glory.

He showed us His love when He gave up His dearly loved Son Jesus to die a tortured, bloody, violent death on the cross to pay the penalty for our sins. It was an act of God's deep love that we cannot completely understand because His unconditional love is limitless. The depth of Jesus' love for His Father compelled Him to willingly give up His life on the cross! His Father brought Him back from the dead after three days, and now Jesus reigns in heaven and sits at the right hand of God, loving us with an everlasting love.

This is supernatural life of limitless love. The Apostle Paul, who knew this love personally, wrote to the people of Ephesus and to us to share this love today.

"And I pray that you, been rooted and established in love, may have power, together with all the saints, to grasp how wide and long and deep is the love of Christ, and to know this love that surpasses knowledge—that you may be filled to the measure of all the fullness of God" (Ephesians 3:18–19).

His greatness no one can fathom!
Psalm 145:3

God shows us His love every day in countless ways. If we pay attention and keep looking for Him everywhere, we'll see His fingerprints all over His glorious creation.

The majestic beauty of Niagara Falls was brought to my attention during a time of private prayer. I was thanking God for His love and mercy and was reminded of His unconditional love. I was humbled trying to fathom His love for me, being fully aware of all my frailties. And while my eyes were still closed in prayer, in my mind, I heard what sounded like loud, pounding water, like a massive waterfall that was unstoppable. The thought of Niagara Falls came to mind. Maybe God wanted me to hear the powerful yet comforting sound as if it was what His love pouring over me would sound like if someone recorded it.

Immediately I recalled a family trip to Niagara Falls as a little girl, hearing the tremendous, almost deafening sound of the falls and experiencing the breathtaking beauty of it all.

I wanted to hear that sound again, so I looked up videos of Niagara Falls online and watched and listened to several of them. I even turned up the volume on my laptop and closed my eyes. It all came back, and, in a new sense, I was in awe at the wonder of God's creation and how He speaks to us through it. It was an awakening of my soul, and I was overjoyed. I was drinking in the thought that God's love for me and for all His children is infinite and unchangeable. God was mentoring me at that moment. Our mentors bring spiritual insight and lead us into eye-opening truths of who God is. We become enlightened and begin to discover beautiful treasures of truth for ourselves. Hopefully, the nurturing grows the passionate fruit of lifelong learning and seeking God.

Think of this: *every second*, more than 3,100 tons of water flow over the three majestic falls that make up Niagara Falls. It is not a coincidence that it's like another trinity, the trinity of its Creator: God the Father, God the

Son, and God the Holy Spirit. God created the beauty and the force of the massive waterfalls, and His love for His children is an even greater force than tons of pounding water.

Women Who Follow Jesus Don't Just Rock Cradles

*"...they had followed Jesus from Galilee
to care for his needs."*
Matthew 27:55

Women who follow Jesus don't just rock cradles. We are meant to rock the world with all the love and hope and Holy Spirit power inside of each one of us. We are global, from every tribe, tongue, generation, and nation. We were born to nurture, born to be wild with the power of His love, all for the glory of God.

Women who follow Jesus are fully aware of broken places in our souls and prayerfully run to the Father, hopefully *before* we hit rock bottom. Women who follow Jesus have all the privileges of living a supernatural life: the forgiveness of sin, unconditional love, powerful prayers that move mountains, and the grace of God that melts our hearts with His loving kindness. He loves, provides, protects, and keeps all His promises since He is "faithful in all he does" (Psalm 33:4).

He has equipped us to be nurturers and to be nurtured. It's common for women to easily shed tears at a sad story, be quick to hug a friend, cook or feed somebody a meal, and become a Mama Bear if she senses danger is near her children or close friends. That's instinctive for us.

But it seems like too many Christian women are having an identity crisis. Below the surface, we're not sure who we really are anymore. We're confused because the world insists, through all sorts of media marketing, that we must look like the women airbrushed on magazine covers who stare back at us while we're in the checkout line at the grocery store. The world tells us our value comes from having a youthful, physically fit appearance. And somehow, the lie works into our minds that if we can gain some sort of celebrity status, we'll receive all the value and affirmation we have been craving. Sadly, such desires will never be satisfied because our value doesn't come from people; it comes from the limitless love of Jesus. There is only one true celebrity, Jesus, and it is His fame we should be promoting. "Yes, Lord...your name and renown are the desires of our hearts" (Isaiah 26:8).

Our identity is not in what we do. It's who we are—women who follow Jesus. And it's a very high calling! Look at the roles women who followed Jesus played in the Bible. We can read in John 4:7–42 the testimony of the Samaritan woman who went to a well to draw water and discovered Jesus sitting there. He offered her living water. After her life-changing encounter, she was transformed, acknowledging her sin and His power to save her from her sins. Immediately she left her jar of water and headed into town to tell the people about Jesus, calling Him "the man who told me everything I ever did." This woman was an evangelist! She knew God's love and wanted a whole town to know it, too. Many townspeople were saved when the woman witnessed to them. Then they went out to meet Jesus. In fact, they told her, "We no longer believe just because of what you said; now we have heard for ourselves, and we know that this man really is the Savior of the world" (v. 42).

There's a familiar story in Luke 10:38–42 of two sisters, Mary and Martha.

Women who follow Jesus don't just rock cradles.

Matthew 27:55

They were close friends of Jesus. He loved and respected women. Just picture being a close friend of Jesus, walking along with Him, and having Him come to your home for dinner. That's a high honor in itself! Martha was hospitable and kindly invited Jesus to come to her home. When she began to prepare everything for a meal, she became anxious and was "distracted by all the preparations" (v. 40) while her sister Mary literally "sat at the Lord's feet listening to what He said" (v. 33). Martha became frustrated, went over to Jesus, complaining, and said, "Lord, don't you care that my sister has left me to do the work by myself? Tell her to help me!" (v. 40)

His response? "Martha, Martha, you are worried and upset about many things—but only one thing is needed. Mary has chosen what is better, and it will not be taken away from her" (vv. 41–42).

Wait. In Scripture, we're exhorted to "Share with God's people who are in need. Practice hospitality" (Romans 12:13). Yes, we are, and Martha was generous and loving to invite Jesus to her home. But her emotions escalated when she turned her eyes toward herself, perhaps striving to make a perfect presentation of her hostess skills. Mary sat still at His feet in calmness and focused on Him and His words.

One sister was hungry for Jesus to abundantly feed and nourish her soul; the other was striving to please Him with her good works of hospitality. He loved them both unconditionally. He knows our weaknesses and gives us grace.

Jesus loves His Church so much He gave up His life to birth it. "Be imitators of God, therefore, as dearly loved children and live a life of love, just as Christ loved us and gave himself up for us as a fragrant offering and sacrifice to God" (Ephesians 5:1–2). Do we love His global Church so much we're willing to deny ourselves and follow Him?

During the days of the Bible, the women who followed Jesus had a significant impact on His ministry. These women knew He was the One who healed their bodies and their souls. They worshiped Him as they went and even gave money to His ministry. "Jesus traveled from one town and village to another, proclaiming the good news of the kingdom of God. The Twelve were with Him and women who had been cured of evil spirits and diseases… These women were helping to support them out of their own means" (Luke 8:1–3).

Women were present at the horrific crucifixion of Jesus. "Many women were there, watching from a distance. They had followed Jesus from Galilee to care for His needs" (Matthew 27:55). Later that evening, they went to the tomb as the huge stone was rolled over the entrance.

Three days later, several women who returned with perfumes and spices to anoint Jesus' body discovered the stone was rolled away, and the tomb was empty. An angel told them Jesus was alive again, as He said would happen. And again, it was women who carried the message of the empty tomb back to the "Eleven and all the others" (Luke 24:10).

After Jesus ascended into heaven, the disciples returned to the upper room where they were staying in Jerusalem. "They all joined together constantly in prayer along with the women and Mary the mother of Jesus, and with his brothers" (Acts 1:14). The women were fearless in meeting to pray and remained faithful as His followers.

These women were also willing to be persecuted along with the other disciples. "On that day, a great persecution broke out against the church at Jerusalem, and all except the apostles were scattered throughout Judea and Samaria. Godly men buried Stephen and mourned deeply for him. But Saul began to destroy the church. Going from house to house, he dragged off men and women and put them in prison" (Acts 8:1–3).

Christ's faithful followers were a community that grew into the church! They denied themselves daily, took up their own crosses, and followed Jesus (Luke 9:23). The women were nurturers of their community, including Jesus. He nurtured His followers as their Holy Shepherd. It's the same for us today; our relationship with Him is supernatural. We have a glorious identity as women who follow Jesus, "The Lord is my shepherd, I shall not be in want" (Psalm 23:1).

Truth never changes. Scripture never changes. God never changes. "Jesus Christ is the same yesterday and today and forever" (Hebrews 13:8). That is our security. And I believe that's what I witnessed in the women who were my mentors. Through it all, He was their Rock.

"We're Having a Party!"

All the days of the oppressed are wretched, but the
cheerful heart has a continual feast.
Proverbs 15:15

Every day we must decide if we're going to host a pity party—in our hearts and minds—or a feast of joy. It's a mindset. It's faith. Or unbelief. I confess I have hosted a few pity parties, and no one ever comes! I am sure I was not trusting God in those situations.

But seriously, will we believe God's promises so we can overcome self-centered thinking of hopelessness? Even if we're experiencing painful brokenness and persecution, He tells us, "We are more than conquerors through him who loved us" (Romans 8:37). Look, He helps us in our storms and calls us overcomers. "You dear children are from God and have overcome them, because the one who is in you is greater than one who is in the world" (1 John 4:4).

Over and over, we can read throughout Scripture God is glorified when His children are thankful and joyful towards Him. "Be joyful always; pray continually; give thanks in all circumstances, for this is God's will for you in Christ Jesus" (1 Thessalonians 6:16–18).

He deeply loves His people. "As the Father has loved me, so I have loved you. Now remain in my love. I have told you this so that my joy may be in you and that your joy may be complete" (John 15:9, 11).

God loves to see us celebrate Him. It's worship! Again, the verse "...the cheerful heart has a continual feast" (Proverbs 15:15). According to the NIV Study Bible Commentary, when we have a cheerful heart, it states, "Life is as joyful and satisfying as the days of a festival."

It's our attitude that's described here, and the fruit is a festival-like life!

In Scripture, a festival was considered a celebration with people, food, and drink. God told the Israelites, "Three times a year you are to celebrate a festival to me" (Exodus 23:14). They were to celebrate God's goodness to them.

The first festival was the Feast of the Unleavened Bread, commemorating the mass exodus out of bondage in Egypt. Then God commanded, "Celebrate the Feast of the Harvest with the firstfruits of the crops you sow in your field" (Exodus 23:16). This was also called the Feast of Weeks because it was held seven weeks after the first festival. They were to celebrate the blessings of the first harvest in the promised land. The third festival was The Feast of the Ingathering (Exodus 23:16). This was also called the Feast of the Tabernacles or Booths because they lived in temporary shelters when God brought them out of Egypt; they celebrated that they had new homes and rejoiced in the produce of the land where He brought them.

They gave God glory in their festivals for His generous provision! What about us today? Do we have any reason to be cheerful today and maybe even plan an impromptu, informal type of festival to the Lord?

God wants us to celebrate His love for us. He celebrates us and "delights in the well-being of His servants" (Psalm 35:27). The Israelites suffered through so many painful trials as we all do, but God never lets us go, and He carries us when we need His strength to persevere.

When Ezra read the recently recovered Book of the Law of Moses to the Israelites, they wept over their past sins. "Nehemiah said, 'Go and enjoy choice food and sweet drinks, and send some to those who have nothing prepared. This day is sacred to our Lord. Do not grieve, for the joy of the Lord is your strength'" (Nehemiah 8:10).

It's the same for us today! When we sorrowfully repent of our sins, He forgives us. What follows repentance is joy! Our thankfulness and joy in God give us strength, energy, and encouragement. Think about it. We're energized when we're joyful. We should celebrate it.

I mentioned earlier in this book that my mother, had a cheerful heart, and she could make anything a festival. However, she had tragic circumstances fall on her and had good reasons to be grumpy, depressed, self-centered, bitter, and the hostess of many pity parties. Her husband walked out the door one day and abandoned her and their five children. He left a trail of broken hearts in all of us in different ways, but Mom rose to the occasion to hold us together with her love and joyful attitude.

If we stopped for ice cream and sat under an umbrella outside the ice cream shop to devour the creamy treats, she'd say, "We're having a party!" Or, if we were eating her homemade sandwiches at the beach, she'd say the same thing. As we were often playing golf and eating the famous Biltmore Golf Course (Coral Gables, Florida) huge hot dogs "between nines" at the halfway house, she'd say, "We're having a party!"

Her life was a continual feast, and she wanted my four siblings and me to learn that if we had a cheerful heart, we could have lives like that, too. She was just simply grateful, and it was easy for her to celebrate life!

We all have that choice. What do we want for our families? Friends? Community? It's a gift of grace from God to be thankful, joyful, unselfish, and to love unconditionally, in spite of our circumstances. And since it's possible, we can ask God for it because "no good thing does He withhold from those whose walk is upright... blessed is the one who trusts in Him!" (Psalm 84:11).

Mom obviously made a choice to hold her beloved family together, and she really loved us all unconditionally. She had so much pain from their divorce, and I believe she always had a lingering sting because he didn't just abandon her but his whole family. Despite it all, by the grace of God, what consistently came out of her was an abundance of love, laughter, and the joy of life! She was as joyful as a festival to me!

A cheerful
heart has a
continual feast
Proverbs 15:15

Driving Out the Darkness

"My God turns my darkness into light."
Psalm 18:28

When we find ourselves driving down the dark road of anxiety, it means we've taken a wrong turn—we've let our minds wander into a dark place. It's all the old baggage we've stuffed in the back seat of our minds that is steering us in the wrong direction: regret, unforgiveness, reliving the *emotions* of the past, uncontrolled thoughts, temptation to revive addictive behavior, and self-centered control issues. It's a dark drive on a dark road because there are no lights of hope on that street! The anxiety is in our heads, and our senses are dulled.

But God knows our struggles. He is the one who will show us how to turn on our headlights—yes, headlights—so we can take thoughts captive and wake ourselves out of a spiritually blind, self-centered stupor. It's not safe to drive in a stupor: you tend to stumble and run off the road!

The cure is to open our Bibles and ask God to make His truth and promises to shine the light on the darkness. "Your word is a lamp to my feet and a light to my path" (Psalm 119:105). We must pray!

The moment we stop allowing ourselves to be distracted by worldly chatter (social media) and put our eyes on the radiant road to freedom in Christ, He will open our spiritual eyes and light our way! All the safe boundaries—just like the metallic stripes on the road—will shine brightly.

When we approach darkness on our travels and persevere in faith, God will shine brighter than every dark place! Every time! "The path of the righteous is like the first gleam of dawn, shining ever brighter till the full light of day" (Proverbs 4:18).

If this sounds like I'm very familiar with struggling with uncontrolled thoughts and old ways of thinking, it's because I'm speaking from personal experience. I know I'm not alone in this kind of spiritual battle. I came to the truth that this stronghold was not glorifying to my Lord, and so I began tenaciously seeking His face daily in constant prayer and Bible study. I knew He would be the healer and deliverer of what I was asking; God is the Creator of light! I am confident He is the One for whatever is needed to get me through the storms when they come.

I've seen this kind of faith in my mentors. When darkness troubled their souls, they battled in prayer and, at times, called me to help them pray their way through the darkness back into the light. It was reciprocal and precious and powerful—every time!

So, sure, there will be dark, rough patches of road that show up on our journey, but God does not want us to put on the brakes in spiritual darkness, so we can stay there and let the darkness steer us into a dead end. Why? "When Jesus spoke again to the people, He said, 'I am the light of the world. Whoever follows Me will never live in darkness but will have the light of life'" (John 8:12).

Jesus finished the work His Father sent Him to do here on earth, which was to take the sins of the world onto Himself and destroy the works of the devil (1 John 3:8). Before He returned to His throne at the right hand of God the Father in heaven, He commissioned His disciples, and all who would become children of God, to carry on the work of shining His light on the earth.

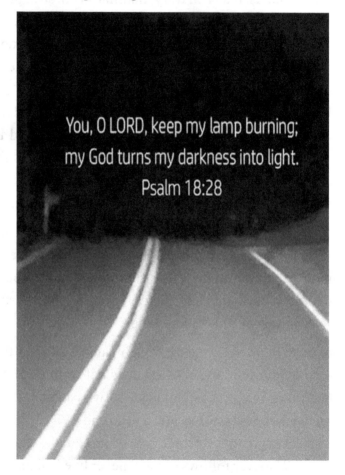

You, O LORD, keep my lamp burning;
my God turns my darkness into light.
Psalm 18:28

These are His words: "You are the light of the world. A city on a hill cannot be hidden. Neither do people light a lamp and put it under a bowl. Instead, they put it on its stand, and it gives light to everyone in the house. In the same way, let your light shine before men, that they may see your good works and glorify your Father in heaven" (Matthew 5:16).

Jesus suffered torturous darkness and death on the cross and rose to the light of life again so we could have life in Him. He is constantly inviting us to follow Him, and He is the one who will *keep our lamp burning and turn our darkness into light.*

Hallelujah!

The Devil Doesn't Have a Shield but We Do!

"...take up the shield of faith... you can extinguish all the flaming arrows of the evil one."
Ephesians 6:16

Let's keep it real. We all are struggling with something, whether it's mental, emotional, relational, or physical. We're longing for a breakthrough or a healing of some sort, for ourselves or for someone else.

If we're seeing our troubles through the eyes of faith, then we know "our struggle is not against flesh and blood, but against the rulers, against the authorities, against the powers of this dark world and against the spiritual forces of evil in the heavenly realms" (Ephesians 6:2).

Whatever the case, if we're looking at our struggles through spiritual eyes, the eyes of God's truth, we can see it's *not* hopeless. Jesus told His disciples to always pray and not give up (Luke 18:1). That's what I saw in my mentors. They struggled, experienced heartache, disappointment, and kept going. They didn't lose their smiles during trials and remained interested in the lives of others.

They overcame by going to the Lord on their knees and in their prayer closets, covering their situations, families, and friends with fervent, faithful prayer. It was a lifestyle and a daily activity; they enjoyed ongoing conversations with the Lord. Nothing was too small or too big to bring to the Lord in prayer.

If the generation behind us sees our **PASSION** to **PRAY ABOUT EVERYTHING** we will have shown them a weapon of warfare that cannot be resisted.

Luke 18:1

As I followed their example, I found this truth out for myself countless times. One experience happened several years ago when I was working as a public relations officer at a Christian school. Part of my job description was to greet each family in the car line as they drove up to the front door of the school. I greeted the parents and the kids with an enthusiastic "Good morning!" while I opened the car doors so the students could step out. I closed the car door as the student entered the building and told the parent to have a blessed day.

Usually, the parents had a cup of coffee in their cup holder—it was before eight a.m.—and sometimes, the kids were sleepy or frowning. But I didn't let that stop me from smiling and greeting loudly and even doing a few dance steps if there was music blasting from their cars.

I received many compliments from parents, and the kids seemed to enjoy the lively, uninhibited greeting. But when a parent asked me, "How are you able to be so energetic so early in the morning, and with every car?" I said that I prayed on my way to work every day, asking God to help me by filling me with energy and vitality so I could encourage the families who show up every morning. The parent who asked me that question immediately said, "Wow! I wish my wife would pray for energy and vitality!" True story.

Matthew 4:1–11 and Luke 4:1–13 describe Jesus' battle with the devil. Three times the devil tempted Jesus to bow to him for material wealth, but his fiery darts fizzled out every time Jesus hurled Scripture right back at him. Wow. Jesus spoke verses, and the devil left. Turned away. Scripture repelled him.

Here's the game-changer: the devil doesn't have a shield, but we do! I can't find it in Scripture where he has a shield to protect himself. I only know he is a liar and has devilish minions (John 8:44).

In countless verses, God is described as a shield, "Do not be afraid, Abram. I am your shield" (Genesis 15:1); David prayed, "For surely, O Lord, you bless the righteous; you surround them with your favor as a shield" (Psalm 5:12); "He is a shield to those who take refuge in him" (Proverbs 30:5).

And of course, (Ephesians 6:10–18) describes the full armor of God as our spiritual shield so we can resist all onslaughts of the enemy. We have all the spiritual arsenals we need, which includes prayer: "be alert and always keep on praying for all the saints" (v. 18).

Think about prayer for a moment. We must deny ourselves to pray. It's seen as *work* for some people to stop and to pray, but for God's faithful ones, it's a labor of love for God's glory and the good of others. We pray because we know the truth; the Holy Spirit of God makes our prayers powerful. But we've got to pray to see this promise fulfilled: "The prayer of the righteous is powerful and effective" (James 5:16).

My mentors left me with powerful, life-giving legacies. If the generation behind us sees our passion to pray about everything, we will have shown them a weapon of warfare that cannot be resisted.

AFTERWORD
He Won't Leave Us

"I will instruct you and teach you in the way you should go;
I will counsel you and watch over you."

Psalm 32:8

Spiritual mentoring grows beautiful, supernatural friendships when they are rooted in the word of God, with Jesus as the Absolute Master Gardener and Nurturer. Yes, God is the Master Nurturer of His children. Think about His gentle yet powerful love for us as He nurtures us throughout our lives!

For months I poured out my heart in these pages as bittersweet memories came back to me. I was full of joyful as well as grieving tears sitting in front of my laptop and being reminded just how much these women loved me unconditionally! They knew I loved them unconditionally, too. God knows I miss talking to them, and I remain incredibly grateful to Him for bringing these three women into my life! As I gathered my thoughts and looked at countless photos, I could almost hear God saying to me, "I'm reminding you I love you unconditionally, I'm with you, and I know what you need. I am continuing to pour it out to you! Keep going; there's more."

Psalm 32:8 is one of the verses I pray back to God

daily. The first time it caught my attention was when I was working on a big project years ago and I wanted His guidance. I thought it covered everything I was needing: His teaching, His instruction, His counseling, and His care for me. And now, as I bring this manuscript to a close, He's bringing it back to me in a new way.

During this whole process of writing, He has been plowing deeper furrows into my heart and planting seeds for more fruit for His Kingdom. He wants a great harvest of souls, transformed and motivated by an abiding love for Him and a love for people. As described in Matthew 9:36–38, Jesus is "having compassion on the crowds of the harassed and helpless...he said to his disciples, 'The harvest is plentiful, but the workers are few. Ask the Lord of the harvest, therefore, to send out workers into his harvest field.'"

This describes spiritual nurturing. Pray, ask God to direct you as you go out into the harvest field to reach out to another woman for coffee, or lunch, or a playdate with your little ones. Just reach out to encourage each other and watch what The Lord of the Harvest will do.

ABOUT THE AUTHOR

Polly Balint is passionate about pointing other women to Christ so they could experience the supernatural, unconditional love of Jesus for themselves, as she abundantly enjoys. She's led Bible studies for women for decades: in churches, in the marketplace, and during conferences. She hosted a year-round women's study in her own neighborhood for nine years. She's the author of a trilogy of devotional books, a former freelance writer for national magazines, and a featured lifestyle writer for newspapers in South Florida and Georgia. She hosted a radio talk show at a local Christian radio station, interviewing difference-makers in the community. Polly and her husband, Don, live in Canton, Georgia, and have two beautiful adult daughters, one wonderful son-in-law, one hilarious grandson, and one sweet rescue dog. For more information, visit pollybalint.blogspot.com, Instagram @pollybalint, or contact her at authorpollybalint@gmail.com.

CPSIA information can be obtained
at www.ICGtesting.com
Printed in the USA
JSHW011634310722
28657JS00007B/17